W9-DFT-391

WORLD ALMANAC®
LIBRARY OF THE
Middle East

CONFLICTS
of the Middle East

South Huntington Pub. Lib.
145 Pidgeon Hill Rd.
Huntington Sta., N.Y. 11746

David Downing

Academic Consultant:
William Ochsenwald
Professor of History, Virginia Polytechnic Institute
and State University

Gareth Stevens
Publishing

Please visit our website at: www.garethstevens.com
For a free color catalog describing our list of high-quality books and multimedia programs,
call 1-800-542-2595 (USA) or 1-800-387-3178 (Canada). Our Fax: 1-877-542-2596.

Library of Congress Cataloging-in-Publication Data

Downing, David, 1946-
    Conflicts of the Middle East / David Downing.
       p. cm. — (World Almanac Library of the Middle East)
    Includes bibliographical references and index.
    ISBN-10: 0-8368-7333-5 — ISBN-13: 978-0-8368-7333-7 (lib. bdg.)
    ISBN-10: 0-8368-7340-8 — ISBN-13: 978-0-8368-7340-5 (softcover)
    1. Arab-Israeli conflict—Juvenile literature. I. Title. II. Series.
  DS119.7.D688   2006
  956.04—dc22   2006014028

J 956.04
Downing

First published in 2007 by
World Almanac® Library
1 Reader's Digest Road
Pleasantville, NY 10570-7000, USA

This edition ©2007 by World Almanac® Library.

Produced by Discovery Books
Editors: Geoff Barker, Amy Bauman, Paul Humphrey, and Gianna Quaglia
Series designer: Sabine Beaupré
Designer and page production: Ian Winton
Photo researcher: Rachel Tisdale
Maps: Stefan Chabluk
Academic Consultant: William Ochsenwald,
    Professor of History, Virginia Polytechnic Institute and
    State University
World Almanac® Library editorial direction: Mark J. Sachner
World Almanac® Library editor: Alan Wachtel
World Almanac® Library art direction: Tammy West
World Almanac® Library production: Jessica Morris

Picture credits: cover: Spencer Platt/Getty Images; p. 5: Nicholas Kamm/AFP/Getty Images;
p. 6: General Photographic Agency/Getty Images; p. 8: CORBIS; p.11: Sebastian Bolesch/
Still Pictures; p. 12: London Express/Getty Images; p. 15: Keystone/Getty Images; p. 16:
David Rubinger/Time Life Pictures/Getty Images; p.19: Ramzi Haidar/AFP/Getty Images;
p. 21: Potter/Express/Getty Images; p. 23: John Isaac/Still Pictures; p. 24: Bill Foley/Time
Life Pictures/Getty Images; p. 26: Keystone/Getty Images; p. 27: Mike Nelson/AFP/Getty
Images; p. 29: Thomas Coex/AFP/Getty Images; p. 32: Peter Turnley/CORBIS; p. 35:
AFP/Getty Images; p. 36: CWO Alek Malhas/U.S. Marine Corps.; p. 39: Scott Peterson/
Getty Images; p. 41: Patrick Baz/AFP/Getty Images; p. 42: Awad Awad/AFP/Getty Images

Printed in the United States of America

2 3 4 5 6 7 8 9 10 09 08

CONTENTS

Cover: *Iraqi civilians flee their home in Basra in March 2003. The city was the focus of fighting between Ba'ath Party loyalist troops and U.S. forces.*

The Middle East

The term *Middle East* has a long and complex history. It was originally used by the British in the nineteenth century to describe the area between the Near East (those lands gathered around the eastern end of the Mediterranean Sea) and Britain's empire in India. This area included Persia (later Iran), the **Mesopotamian provinces** of the **Ottoman Empire** (later Iraq), and the eastern half of Saudi Arabia. It was centered on the Persian Gulf.

The British had separate military commands for the Near East and the Middle East, but between the two world wars these commands were joined together. The new Middle East

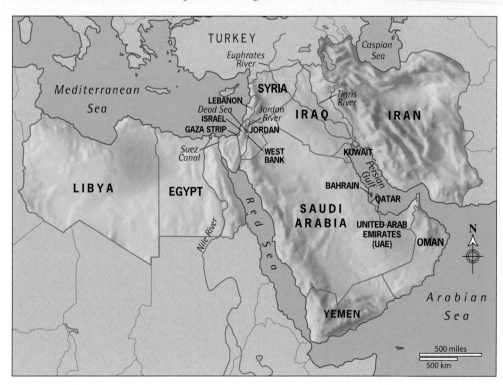

This map shows the fifteen countries of the Middle East that will be discussed in this book, as well as the West Bank and the Gaza Strip.

Oil wells set alight by Saddam Hussein's armies in retreat from Kuwait in 1991. Oil is a source of wealth—and, therefore, a source of conflict—in the region.

Command included the old Near East Command, and stretched from Iran to Libya. After World War II, the term *Near East* fell out of use. In this series, the Middle East is taken to include these fifteen countries: Libya and Egypt in north Africa; the Mediterranean coast states of Israel, Lebanon, and Syria; Jordan, Iraq, and Iran; and the Arabian Peninsula countries of Bahrain, Kuwait, Saudi Arabia, United Arab Emirates, Oman, Yemen, and Qatar. It also includes the Arab Palestinian territories of the Gaza Strip and the West Bank, which have had varying degrees of autonomy under Israeli occupation since 1967.

Why is this region important? Two reasons stand out. One, the Middle East was the original source of civilization, and the three great religions of **Christianity**, **Judaism**, and **Islam** all grew up there. The area includes Israel, the state of the Jewish people, and a significant proportion of the world's Muslims. Two, the Middle East has two-thirds of the fuel that keeps the rest of the world running—oil. For these two reasons alone, the affairs of the Middle East—its peoples and resources, religions and politics, revolutions and wars—are of vital interest to everyone on the planet.

This book looks at the conflicts that have scarred the history of the modern Middle East. The sources of conflict in the region will be outlined, and then the different types of conflict—wars of independence and conquest, wars over territory and resources, **civil wars** and **terrorism**—will be examined in detail. In conclusion, the book will assess the likely sources of future conflict.

CHAPTER 1

Sources of Conflict

Universal Sources of Conflict

The Middle East has seen many conflicts in the last century. There have been violent revolutions and long-running civil wars, wars between countries of the region, and wars involving countries from outside the region.

Some sources of conflict are the same everywhere. Throughout history, on every continent, the same patterns have been repeated, both between and within countries. Power-hungry political leaders have led their parties or countries into war with their neighbors, inventing whatever excuses they felt they needed. Others have gone to war in support of their religious beliefs or political ideals. The Crusaders who invaded the Middle East between the eleventh and fourteenth centuries were examples of the former, the French revolutionary armies of the 1790s examples of the latter. Disputes over the positioning of frontiers and the ownership of national resources have also given rise to conflict on numerous occasions.

British armored cars on patrol in the deserts of Iraq around 1922. Western interference during the colonial period sowed the seeds of future conflict throughout the region.

6

Western Intervention in Iran

Iran was never a colony, but Western powers—Britain between the wars and the United States after World War II—exerted enormous influence over Iran's economy and political life. When the **nationalist** Prime Minister Mohammad Mossadegh tried to take control of Iran's Western-owned oil industry in 1951–1953, the U.S. Central Intelligence Agency organized his overthrow. Although a new prime minister was put in place, it was the pro-Western **shah**, Muhammad Reza Pahlavi, who really ran the country. For the next quarter century, the United States supported the shah, who ruled his country as a virtual **dictator**. Such Western interventions in Middle Eastern affairs were neither forgotten nor forgiven by most ordinary Middle Easterners.

Conflicts Arising from Colonial Rule

Some sources of conflict have been restricted to particular parts of the world. Over recent centuries, large areas of the globe—including the Middle East—have been ruled, either directly or indirectly, by a number of **colonial** powers. These powers included several European countries, the United States, Russia, and Japan. In the twentieth century, local objections to colonial rule became a major source of conflict, and this led to many wars of independence. There were many such struggles in the Middle East, most notably in Egypt, Syria, and Iraq.

Between the 1940s and 1970s, colonial rule mostly came to an end. In many cases, however, what the colonial powers left behind—badly drawn borders, governments with little popular backing, economies with poor prospects—provided new sources of conflict.

The ending of colonial rule was also, in many cases, much less complete than it looked. In many of their former colonies, the rich countries continued to control large sectors of industry and agriculture. As such, they had an enormous influence on the success or failure of the newly independent country. This often soured relations between the richer countries and the leaders of the poorer countries. It also created conflict between those who benefited from the links with the richer countries and those who did not.

Finally, the richer countries have sometimes taken steps to defend economic interests that date from the colonial period. They have used their **intelligence services** and military forces to support their allies in the Middle East and to overthrow those Middle Eastern leaders who posed a threat to their economic and political interests.

Conflicts over Religion or Resources

All these different sources of conflict—those that affected the world as a whole and those that affected the world's ex-colonial regions—can be found in the recent history of the Middle East. Two particular factors, however, are unique to the region.

The first of these factors has to do with religion. The Middle

The Dome of the Rock shrine, on the Temple Mount in Jerusalem, is a site sacred to Muslims, Jews, and Christians. It was built in the seventh century A.D.

East was the birthplace of the three great one-God religions of Judaism, Christianity, and Islam, and all three still play a significant role in the region. The fact that the predominantly Christian countries of the West supervised the creation of a Jewish state—Israel—in the middle of a predominantly Islamic region, is one recipe for potential conflict. The uneasy relationship between traditional Islam and the modern world is another.

The second factor has to do with resources. Disputes over natural resources lie at the heart of Middle Eastern life. Two natural resources dominate everything, one because of its importance to the region, the other because of its importance to the whole world. These are water and oil. Water is crucial to life and growth. Oil is crucial to the economic well-being of the global economy. The growing need for water has created conflict inside the region and with the region's neighbors. It threatens to become an increasing source of conflict in the future. Likewise, the demand for oil has created conflict between the region's countries and dominated its relations with the rest of the world. Oil made the colonial powers reluctant to leave and quick to return.

The Discovery of Middle Eastern Oil

"It will provide all our ships east of Suez with fuel; it will strengthen British influence in these parts. It will make us less dependent on foreign-owned oil fields; it will be some reward for those who have ventured such great sums . . . the only disadvantage is personal to myself—it will prolong my stay here."

Lieutenant A. T. Wilson, writing to his father in May 1908, after witnessing the first major oil discovery in southern Persia [later Iran]. Wilson was the commander of a small British military force sent to protect the oil drillers. Later discoveries of huge oil reserves in many Middle Eastern countries led interested Western countries like Britain and the United States to deploy military forces in the region on a more or less permanent basis. From John Keay's Sowing the Wind *[New York: W.W. Norton, 2003].*

CHAPTER 2

Struggles for Independence

The End of Colonialism

Between the two world wars, the peoples of the Middle East demonstrated a growing desire for independence from their foreign rulers. This desire was expressed in a wide range of ways. Nationalist pamphlets and newspapers were printed, political groups formed, street demonstrations organized. The period also was marked by sporadic outbreaks of violent opposition, but there was only one major rebellion. This took place in Iraq, over three summer months in 1920. It cost about 6,500 lives.

World War II was widely seen as a fight for freedom, and once it was won, colonialism became harder to justify. The British withdrawal from India in 1947—the single most important part of their empire outside the homeland—was a clear sign of the times. Though the British and other European colonial powers sometimes fought to keep their colonial possessions—as the French did in Algeria and Indochina and the British did in Malaya and Kenya, for example—they were fighting a losing battle. By the mid-1970s, colonialism was mostly a thing of the past.

Israel

The first struggle for independence in the Middle East was fought and won by the Jews of Palestine in 1947–1949. This was surprising, because as recently as 1918, the Jews had only formed 8 percent of Palestine's population. Most of the Jews in Palestine in 1947 were newcomers to the region, having arrived, mostly from Europe, during the previous thirty years.

Kurdish Independence?

The one large **ethnic** group in the Middle East that has not received independence is the Kurds. The Kurds, who now number around 25 million, live in an area that takes in large parts of Turkey, Iran, and Iraq, and a small area of Syria. There were plans for an independent Kurdistan after World War 1, but the revival of Turkey in the early 1920s prevented their being implemented. Since then, various Kurdish groups have fought sporadic military campaigns against the governments of Turkey, Iraq, and Iran, but without any lasting success.

Since the 2003 U.S.-led war in Iraq and the subsequent occupation, the Kurds in Iraq have enjoyed a large degree of self-government. This may continue once the occupation has ended, but if a new Iraqi government refuses to allow this level of self-government, the Iraqi Kurds may try to leave Iraq and set up their own independent state. Should they succeed in doing so, Kurds in Turkey, Iran, and Syria might try to join them. The consequences of such a Kurdish independence struggle, although hard to predict, would certainly be wide-reaching.

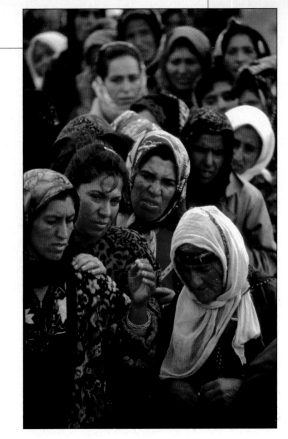

They were encouraged to come by the **Balfour Declaration**. This was Britain's promise to look with favor on "the establishment in Palestine of a national home for the Jewish people." During the years of British **mandate rule** (1920–1948), the Jewish population in Palestine rose sharply, reaching about 31 percent of the total. As the Jewish population and Jewish purchase of land both increased, so did Arab resentment.

Kurdish refugees from Iraq gather in a camp in Iran. The Kurdish people have been scattered over many countries of the Middle East, and some have fled to Europe to avoid persecution.

During World War II, the Palestinian Jews sided with the British against Nazi Germany, but once the war was over, they began pushing the British mandate authorities for a country of their own. In 1947, as tension and violence between Palestinian Jews and Palestinian Arabs grew, the British gave up searching for a solution that satisfied everybody and directed the problem to the **United Nations (UN)**. The UN voted to **partition** the territory, creating two separate countries—one for the Arabs and one for the Jews. The Jews accepted the partition plan. The Arabs, however, rejected it, believing that the whole region was theirs. They also rejected the way it was done, with less than half the land going to their 65 percent of the population.

Violence between the two communities escalated into full-scale war. The better-organized Israelis soon secured most of the land allocated to the new Jewish country as well as much

Women have long played an active part in Israel's armed forces. Here, female members of the Jewish defense force, the Haganah, practice drill routines in the British mandate of Palestine in 1938.

of the land allotted to the Arabs. The ever-present violence, including incidents like the Deir Yassin massacre in which over two hundred Arab villagers were murdered by the Irgun, Jewish terrorist group, frightened many other Arabs into fleeing their land and homes. Other, less well-known atrocities were later committed by both sides. Although many Arabs left Israel, thousands chose to stay; they live there even today as Israeli Arabs and represent approximately one-fifth of the population.

A Forecast

"I am certain that the world will judge the Jewish state by what it shall do with the Arabs."

Chaim Weitzmann, an early Zionist leader and the first president of Israel. From David Downing and Gary Herman's War Without End, Peace Without Hope: Thirty Years of the Arab-Israeli Conflict *[New English Library, 1978].*

In May 1948, the British finally left. The new state of Israel was founded, whereupon five Arab states — Egypt, Lebanon, Transjordan, Syria, and Iraq — sent their armies in to destroy it. They too proved no match for the new Israelis. When the war ended in 1949, Israel controlled about 75 percent of the old mandate territory, and 725,000 Palestinian Arabs had become **refugees**. Israel had secured independence, but not the acceptance of its neighbors. The war had also left Egypt in control of the Gaza Strip and Jordan in control of the West Bank, areas designated by the UN partition plan as part of the Palestinian Arab state.

The Struggle for Egypt's Independence

Egypt was given a form of independence in 1922, but everyone knew that, ultimately, the British remained in control. British troops were based in the **Suez Canal Zone**, which passes through the northeast corner of Egypt, and the Royal Navy was never far away. If the Egyptian king or the Egyptian government disagreed with the British high commissioner, it was always the latter's view that counted. Most educated Egyptians hated this state of affairs. Egypt's president Gamal Abdel Nasser (1918–1970) remembered shouting "O God Almighty, may a calamity overtake the English" as British planes flew overhead during his youth in the 1930s.

A Declaration of Independence

"At the moment, some of your brethren, the sons of Egypt, are now taking over the Egyptian Suez Canal Company, and directing it. We have taken this decision to restore part of the glories of the past and to safeguard our national dignity and pride."

President Nasser, concluding his speech to the Egyptian people on July 26, 1956, in which he announced the nationalization of the Suez Canal. From Robert Stephens' Nasser [New York: Penguin, 1971].

During World War II, the British turned Egypt into a huge military base. When the war was over, the British remained. The Suez Canal was still important—especially because, even after granting India independence in 1947, the British had vital interests in the Persian Gulf and Southeast Asia. Negotiations between Britain and the Egyptian government over the terms of a British withdrawal dragged on for several years.

The British troops were eventually withdrawn, but British officials still ran the Suez Canal. Ships passing through paid their tolls to the canal's British and French owners, not the Egyptians whose country it crossed. After the 1952 revolution, the new **Arab nationalist** rulers of Egypt were determined to win real independence for their country. When, in July 1956, the United States withdrew an offer to finance a much-needed new dam on the Nile River, President Nasser found a different way to raise the money. He announced that the canal was being taken into Egyptian ownership.

The British and French refused to accept this. They landed troops in the Canal Zone. But they quickly discovered that such blatant colonialism had few supporters. Both the new super-powers—the United States and Soviet Union—opposed them, and the UN insisted on their withdrawal. Egypt had won the right to run the Canal and receive the revenues it generated. For many Egyptians, this victory offered proof that their country was finally independent.

Other Struggles for Independence

Other countries of the Middle East also struggled to gain real independence from the British. Iraq was granted formal independence in 1932, but it was not until 1958 that British influence was ended with the overthrow of the pro-British monarchy and government. Military officers and **Ba'athists** led this revolution and another in 1963, but in both cases, the former soon turned on the latter. It was not until 1968 that the Iraqi Ba'athists seized power on their own.

After their final eviction from Egypt in 1956, the British increased their presence in the Aden Protectorate, a region of what is now known as Yemen. Over the next ten years, local **guerrilla** groups fought a war of independence against them. The British withdrew in 1967, and the People's Republic of South Yemen was founded. This country merged with North Yemen to form the Republic of Yemen in 1990.

Egypt's President Nasser giving a speech in Damascus, Syria, in 1959. Nasser was a charismatic leader who was popular throughout the region.

Israel and the Arab Countries

Two Sides to the Argument

After Israel had established itself, the conflict between Palestinian Jews and Palestinian Arabs turned into a conflict between Israel and the neighboring Arab countries. This seemed an impossible conflict to resolve. The two sides wanted opposite outcomes, and each had good reason for wanting them.

As far as Israelis were concerned, they had every right to their new state. After enduring centuries of **persecution** in Europe, about a third of the Jewish people had perished in the Nazi **Holocaust**. The surviving Jews believed they deserved a home

Israeli soldiers guard their position along the Suez Canal, while watching Egyptian positions on the opposite shore during the 1967, or Six-Day, War.

of their own. And the home they wanted was not just any home; the new Israel occupied some of the same lands as the Jewish state that had flourished in the first millennium B.C. Some Jews had lived there for centuries, and the **Zionist** movement had been arguing for a Jewish homeland in Palestine for over fifty years. In 1947, the Jews had finally been awarded their new country by the United Nations. They felt it was the Arabs who had rejected partition, and they only had themselves to blame for the consequences. Until the Arabs accepted Israel's right to exist, Israel had no intention of dealing with them.

As far as the Arabs were concerned, Palestine was their land and had been for at least thirteen hundred years. They thought the British had no right to promise the Jews a homeland on someone else's land, and the UN had no right to make the Arabs pay for a European Holocaust. The Arabs had rejected—and fought against—partition because they saw it as simple theft. They had lost one war, but they would not accept that the loss was permanent. They would not accept the existence of Israel.

The 1967 War

As the 1960s unfolded, the Arab states grew increasingly confident that they could avenge the defeat of 1948–1949. In the early summer of 1967, Egypt's President Nasser asked the UN to withdraw its troops from the Israeli-Egyptian border, and he closed the Straits of Tiran—Israel's only route to the east—to Israeli shipping.

Israel did not wait for an actual attack. On the morning of June 5, its air force destroyed the Arab air forces on the ground in a series of surprise raids. Deprived of air support, the armies of Egypt, Jordan, and Syria were no match for Israel's tank forces. The Jordanians were forced out of the West Bank and back across the Jordan River, the Egyptians driven back out of the Gaza Strip and across the Suez Canal. Syria lost the Golan Heights. The whole of pre-1947 Palestine was now in Israeli hands.

Paying Someone Else's Debt

"We Arabs did not kill six million Jews or persecute them. Europeans did that. But we Arabs paid the price. I think I'm entitled to say that life has not been very fair to us."

Palestinian leader Yasser Arafat, talking about the Holocaust in Europe and how it paved the way for the creation of Israel.

The 1973 War

Over the next six years, the Arabs tried guerrilla warfare in the West Bank, terrorism against Israeli targets, and sustained artillery fire against the Israeli positions on the Suez Canal. The United States tried to start talks between the two sides. But the basic situation remained unchanged. The Arab states refused to accept Israel, and Israel continued its occupation of those lands allotted to the Palestinian Arabs by the UN partition plan of 1947.

In 1973, on **Yom Kippur**, a Jewish holy day, the Arab countries went back to war. The Arab leaders were no longer confident that Israel could be destroyed, but war seemed their only hope of bringing Israel to the bargaining table. At first, the plan went well. The Egyptian attack across the Suez Canal on October 6 caught the Israelis by surprise, and the Syrians launched a simultaneous attack into northern Israel. Within days, however, the tide had turned. Israel's forces were still more efficient, better-equipped, and more highly-motivated. By October 22, when a ceasefire was called, Israel's forces were driving toward Cairo and Damascus.

Neither the war nor the peace that followed solved anything. But this third defeat finally convinced the Egyptian leadership that Israel could not be beaten. Without Egypt's large army and air force, Arab countries such as Syria, Jordan, and Iraq had even less chance of ever defeating Israel. The Palestinian Arabs were left to fight for themselves, in whatever way they could.

West Bank and Gaza Strip

There were two areas of the original Palestine mandate territory that were not included in the new state of Israel. The Gaza Strip —a thin piece of territory along the Mediterranean coast—was occupied by Egypt in 1949 and administered from Cairo. The West Bank region was joined to Transjordan, which then became Jordan. After Israel occupied both of these territories in 1967, Egypt and Jordan later agreed that they should be joined together to create an independent Palestinian country.

Yasser Arafat

Yasser Arafat (1929–2004) was born in Jerusalem but spent much of his childhood and youth in the Egyptian capital of Cairo. Although he graduated from the University of Cairo as a civil engineer, he spent all of his spare time involved in political activities. He fought as a volunteer in the 1948–1949 Arab-Israeli War and led guerrilla raids into the West Bank in 1967–1968. In 1969, he was elected Chairman of the Palestine Liberation Organization (PLO). After moving the PLO headquarters from Jordan to Lebanon, he led the Palestinian resistance to the Israeli invasion of Lebanon in 1982. After signing a partial peace with Israel in 1993, he became president of the **Palestinian National Authority**. He died in 2004.

Palestinian leader Yasser Arafat (center) walks among his supporters in Beirut during the early days of the 1982 Israeli invasion of Lebanon.

CHAPTER 4

Civil Wars

The civil wars of the modern Middle East have differed greatly in length and intensity. The issues at stake have also varied. Some civil wars have been caused or partly caused by ethnic or religious differences; some have grown out of disagreements over the politics, economics, and cultural impact of such movements as **modernization** and **Westernization**. Some have been caused or partly caused by the huge gaps between the rich and the poor that exist throughout the region.

Yemen When Yemen's civil war started in 1962, North Yemen (now the northern half of the Republic of Yemen) was the most undeveloped country in the Middle East. Few people could read or write, and **slavery** was still common. The country's rulers—called imams—relied on fear to keep the people quiet.

This map shows where civil wars have flared up in the Middle East during the twentieth century.

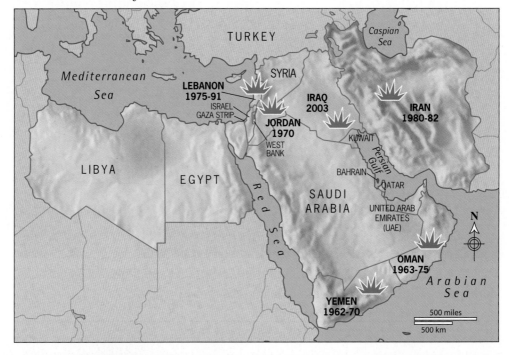

Civilians took to the streets in protests and rioting in Aden, southern Yemen, in October 1965. The British ruled Aden for nearly a century.

These rulers could not, however, prevent the ideas of Arab nationalism from crossing their borders. In September 1962, an alliance of modernizers—army officers, teachers, businessmen, and others—managed to overthrow the imam and seize control of the capital, Sana'a. The imam escaped into the mountains, where his tribal allies lived. The new government abolished slavery and began modernizing business and education.

This was the first time that an Arabian monarch had been overthrown by Arab nationalists, so the whole Middle East was watching to see what happened. Both sides in the Yemen conflict appealed to their allies for help. The new government asked Egypt's President Nasser to send troops, and the imam's supporters—called the Royalists—asked neighboring Saudi Arabia for help. Both countries were willing. As a result, the war lasted for seven years. Despite pouring in more and more troops, the Egyptians were unable to defeat the Royalists in their mountain strongholds. Similarly, the Royalists were unable to shake the nationalists' hold on the capital and on the densely-populated coastal plain.

After the Arabs lost their war with Israel in 1967, Egypt and Saudi Arabia agreed that they could no longer afford to squabble among themselves. Both withdrew their support from their Yemeni allies. The Yemeni Royalists made one last attempt to take Sana'a and failed. By 1970, the fighting was virtually over, and the nationalist republic was firmly established.

Oman The civil war in Oman lasted much longer than that in Yemen and ended in defeat for the country's modernizers. It began in 1963 as a **separatist** movement in the western region of Dhofar but eventually became a countrywide war between **conservatives** and modernizers. In those areas they controlled, modernizing rebels began campaigns against **illiteracy**, slavery, and the **oppression** of women.

By the end of the 1960s, the war had spread to the rest of Oman. This worried the British, who had a long-standing alliance with Sultan Said, the country's dictator. They forced the sultan to step down in favor of his son Qaboos, who introduced some reforms without abandoning any of his dictatorial powers. He also expanded the Omani Army and received substantial military assistance from British Special Forces (the SAS), Pakistani mercenaries, and the Iranian Army. The rebels were finally defeated in 1975, and Sultan Qaboos has remained in power ever since.

Afghanistan

The civil war in Afghanistan, like those in Oman and Yemen, began as a conflict between modernizers and conservatives. The modernizers, led by the local Communist party, soon needed military help from the Soviet Union. The conservatives, led by several **Islamic fundamentalist** parties, then received significant support from the United States and conservative Arab states such as Saudi Arabia. In addition, many individual Muslims from the Middle East traveled to Afghanistan to fight as volunteers against the Soviets.

Osama bin Laden was one of these volunteers. The success of the Islamic fundamentalists in the war against the Soviets—who withdrew their last troops from Afghanistan in 1989—encouraged bin Laden and other war veterans to form a new organization, called al-Qaeda ("the base"). They hoped that they could repeat this defeat of non-Muslim foreign intruders elsewhere in the Muslim world, and particularly in the Middle East. Until 2001, al-Qaeda used war-torn Afghanistan as its base.

Young Palestinian refugees in Amman, Jordan. Large numbers of Palestinians have fled over the border into Jordan during the conflicts with Israel.

Jordan The Jordanian War lasted only ten days, in what Palestinians later called the "Black September" of 1970. On one side, were Jordan's conservative government and army. On the other side, were armed groups recruited from the large Palestinian refugee population in Jordan.

Tensions between the Palestinian groups and their host had been rising steadily since 1967. They were brought to a head in the summer of 1970 by two events. First, Jordan's King Hussein accepted a peace plan for the region that was supported by the United States that the Palestinians loudly rejected. Second, one Palestinian group, the Popular Front for the Liberation of Palestine (PFLP), **hijacked** three Western airliners and held the passengers hostage in the desert near the Jordanian capital. Rather than risk losing control of his own country, King Hussein let his troops loose on the Palestinian fighters.

The first fighting took place on September 15. Four days later, an armed Palestinian unit based in Syria crossed into Jordan. This unit was beaten back by the Jordanian air force. Meanwhile, about 4,000 Palestinians were killed during fighting in and around the refugee camps. By September 25, the government forces were in complete control. Over the next nine months, all armed Palestinians were expelled from Jordan. Most went to Lebanon.

Lebanon The sixteen-year Lebanese Civil War was clearly a religious conflict, in that the primary struggle was between the Christian and Muslim communities. But it was also a struggle for political and economic power. The French, who had at one time governed the territory, had left the Christians with a permanent majority in parliament and most of the country's wealth. The Muslims, who had tried and failed to bring about change by peaceful methods, were, by the mid-1970s, prepared to use force. The arrival of many armed Palestinians from Jordan added to the tension between Christians and Muslims but did not create it.

In late 1975, civil war slowly took hold of Lebanon. The Christians said they would consider a Muslim demand for political reform only when the Palestinians had been ejected from the country. As the arguments dragged on, both sides

Militiamen take cover from sniper fire at a crossing between west and east Beirut in May 1985.

Iran and Iraq

Some historians have called the violence in Iran during 1980–1982 a virtual civil war. This was not a war of open battles. It was fought between the two groups who had overthrown the shah in 1979: the modernizers and the religious conservatives. The modernizers mounted a campaign of bombings against their opponents, killing more than 1,000 people. The conservatives retaliated with mass executions—more than 1,800 people between June and November 1981.

The situation in Iraq following the 2003 overthrow of Saddam Hussein has also been likened to civil war. Much of the violence has been directed against the U.S. and British occupying forces and their Iraqi allies. But there have also been many violent attacks by members of the three major Iraqi communities—the Kurds, the **Sunni** Arabs, and the **Shi'a** Arabs—on each other. Violence has also erupted between different parts of the majority Shi'a community.

began seizing all the territory that they could. By 1976, Lebanon was a patchwork of tiny states ruled by armed **militias**. Many of these tiny states only included a few city blocks. There was almost constant fighting between them.

Over the next sixteen years, several foreign powers—Israel, Syria, the United States, and France—sent troops to Lebanon, but none succeeded in stopping the fighting. Israel's invasion in 1982 forced most of the Palestinian fighters out of Lebanon, but the invasion is also remembered for the massacre of about 2,000 Palestinian civilians at the Sabra and Chatilla refugee camps in southern Beirut. Lebanese Christians carried out the killing, but, as an official Israeli inquiry made clear, Israeli Army units had allowed the massacre to take place.

The civil war continued through the 1980s, with fighting both between and within the two major religious communities. A series of compromises eventually brought the war to an end in 1991. By this time, about 150,000 Lebanese had died, and much of the capital of Beirut was in ruins.

Wars of Conquest

Since World War II there have been few wars in the Middle East waged for the conquest and permanent occupation of another nation's territory. President Nasser of Egypt sent troops to Yemen in 1962, for example, to further those causes—Arab nationalism and modernization—which he believed in, and perhaps also to raise his own personal prestige. He had no intention of making Yemen part of Egypt. President Hafez Assad of Syria sent his troops into Lebanon to influence the outcome of the civil war and to prevent chaos spreading over the border into his own country. He had no intention of making Lebanon part of Syria.

Muammar Gaddafi and "Greater Libya"

Other leaders, however, have been more interested in conquest. Muammar Gaddafi, the leader of Libya since 1969, has sought to spread his influence by this and other means. Maps of Libya published by his own foreign ministry in 1976 showed Algeria, Tunisia, Niger, and Chad as part of "Greater Libya."

In 1973, Gaddafi sent his troops to occupy the Aozou Strip area of northern Chad claiming, over

Colonel Muammar Gaddafi salutes the crowds in May 1976, the year he published maps showing "Greater Libya." Gaddafi is still in power today.

Chadian denials, that he had purchased it. In 1979, as part of his interference in the Chadian Civil War, his troops invaded northern Chad, only to be repulsed. That same summer, Gaddafi, who was a strong opponent of any compromise with Israel, was angered by Egypt's peace deal with Israel and brought Libya and Egypt to the brink of war. Early, in 1980, following a failed attempt at union with Tunisia, Libyan forces mounted a military raid into that country, killing forty-one people.

Around this time, Gaddafi seems to have realized that attempting to spread his influence by military means was not working. He changed tactics. Over the next quarter-century, he used Libya's oil wealth to support foreign political and terrorist groups. He only abandoned this policy in the early twenty-first century when it became apparent that the international community would no longer put up with such activities.

Saddam Hussein's Iraq

Iraq's Saddam Hussein launched two wars of conquest. During his first decade in power (1969–1979) he concentrated on promoting the classic Arab nationalist goals of economic development, true independence, and Arab unity. As part of his call for Arab unity, he stressed the crucial role that a strong Iraq could play in reviving the whole Arab world.

Iraqi President Saddam Hussein (right) and King Hussein of Jordan (left) during a visit by Saddam to Jordan in February 1990. Before his invasion of Kuwait, Saddam was seen as an ally by other Arab nations.

After he became president in 1979, however, a **personality cult** was developed. Saddam's picture was suddenly everywhere. He was the face of Iraq. His ambitions became Iraq's ambitions.

The revolution in neighboring Iran in 1979 presented Saddam with both a threat and an opportunity. The Shi'a revolution in Iran threatened trouble among Iraq's majority Shi'a population; that in turn threatened Saddam's Sunni government. But the chaos in Iran that accompanied that revolution led Saddam to believe that Iran and its rich southern oil fields were there for the taking. If these oil fields were conquered, then Iraq's wealth, and Saddam's influence, would be enormously increased. On September 22, 1980 Saddam launched his armed forces across the border.

After the Iranians halted Iraq's original offensive, the war settled into a virtual stalemate. Month by month, year by year, Iran took back its territory, sending "human waves" of poorly-armed young men against the Iraqi defenses. Hundreds of thousands of soldiers died. Iraqi's army used poison gas against both the Iranians and the northern Iraqi Kurds, who were using the war as an opportunity to launch their own struggle for an independant Kurdish homeland. Unable to make a breakthrough on the ground, the two sides attacked each other's cities with bombers and missiles. In the Persian Gulf, Iraq's air force attacked Iranian tankers and oil terminals.

The Western powers and conservative Arab states like Saudi Arabia and Kuwait all supported Saddam during the Iran-

A Holy War

"You are fighting to protect Islam, and he [Saddam Hussein] is fighting to destroy Islam. At the moment, Islam is confronted by blasphemy [the insulting of God], and you should protect and support Islam. . . . There is no question of peace or compromise, and we shall never have any discussions with them."

Iranian spiritual leader Ayatollah Khomeini, speaking to the Iranian people early in the Iran-Iraq War. From David Downing's Saddam Hussein and Iraq *[Oxford: Heinemann Library, 2003].*

The Hands of Victory is a triumphal arch built by Saddam Hussein to commemorate the war with Iran. The two pairs of crossed swords are made from the guns of dead Iraqi soldiers.

Iraq war because they feared revolutionary Iran. But once the war had reached a stalemate, they had no incentive to intervene. As the former U.S. Secretary of State Henry Kissinger said, it was a pity that both sides couldn't lose. The longer the war went on, the more both would be weakened.

Paying for War with War

One of Saddam's major problems was how to pay for the war against Iran. Rather than raise taxes and risk a rebellion of his own people, he spent the money in his country's treasury. Once this money was gone, he started borrowing, mostly from neighboring countries Kuwait and Saudi Arabia. When mutual exhaustion finally brought the war to an end in 1988, Iraq was deep in debt.

Since Saudi Arabia and Kuwait had supported his war against Iran, Saddam expected them to cancel these debts. They refused. Saddam could have concentrated on getting Iraq back on its feet. But he chose, instead, to launch another war of conquest, seeking to repay his debt by invading oil-rich Kuwait in the summer of 1990.

Most of the world condemned his invasion, and a huge United Nations military coalition—led largely by the United States—was brought together to reverse it. Five weeks of intensive air attacks in January and February 1991 weakened the Iraqi forces, and a few days of fighting on the ground pushed them out of Kuwait. The coalition went no further, however. Saddam was left in power but in a weakened state.

In April 1991, the UN passed Resolution 687, which called upon Iraq to "accept the destruction or removal of all chemical and biological weapons, and ballistic missiles [and]...nuclear material." **Economic sanctions** were introduced against Iraq. These would only be removed when all traces of Saddam's chemical, biological, and nuclear weapons programs had been destroyed. This was to be monitored by teams of **UN weapons inspectors**.

Saddam did destroy these weapons, but he refused to cooperate with the weapons inspectors. In October 1997 the inspectors reported to the UN that Iraq was in breach of Resolution 687. The following year Saddam forced the inspectors

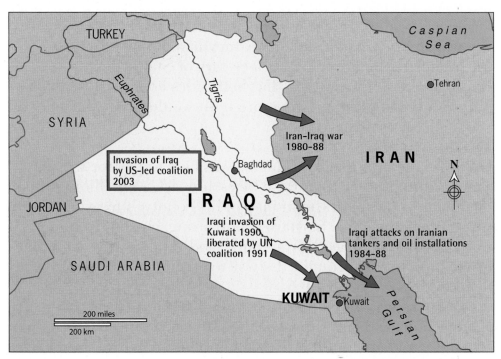

This map shows the three conflicts that Saddam's Iraq was involved in: the war with Iran in the 1980s, the invasion of Kuwait in 1990, and the US-led coalition invasion in 2003.

out of Iraq. Weakened by sanctions, Saddam simply survived and waited for the time when the world would tire of watching him so carefully. Unfortunately for Saddam, the opposite happened. After the September 11, 2001 (or 9/11), terrorist attacks on the United States, the U.S. administration under George W. Bush decided that watching him was no longer enough. Perhaps sensing this, Saddam then began cooperating with the weapons inspectors, but it was too late. In March 2003, Iraq was invaded by a U.S.-led coalition of international forces, and Saddam was driven from power.

A Call for Action

"If Saddam acquires the capability to deliver **weapons of mass destruction**, as he is almost certain to do, then the safety of American troops in the region, the safety of our friends and allies like Israel and the moderate Arab states, and a significant portion of the world's oil supply, will all be put at risk.

"The only acceptable strategy is one that eliminates this possibility. In the short term, this means a willingness to undertake military action, as **diplomacy** is clearly failing. In the long term, it means removing Saddam Hussein and his regime from power. That now needs to become the aim of American foreign policy."

From the open letter sent to President Clinton in January 1998 by eighteen prominent American neoconservatives. These included future Secretary of Defense Donald Rumsfeld, future deputy-Secretary of Defense Paul Wolfowitz, and nine others who held jobs in the first administration of George W. Bush.

The Invasion of Iraq

The invasion of Iraq in March 2003 was not a war of conquest. Neither the United States nor its allies had any interest in a permanent occupation of Iraq. Some commentators argue, however, that the invasion formed part of a U.S. plan for transforming the whole Middle East. The authors of this plan, which formed part of their published "Project for a New American Century," were those influential **neoconservatives** who formed an influential part of President George W. Bush's first administration. This group of right-wing politicians and academics believed that a post-Saddam Iraq could and should be turned into a democratic, U.S. ally. This would encourage other Middle Eastern states to follow the same path, increase regional stability, and ensure the flow of oil. The final success or failure of this plan remains in doubt.

CHAPTER 6

Israel and the Palestinians

The Arab countries had failed to destroy Israel. They had failed to win control of any part of the original Palestine for its Arab inhabitants. By the end of the 1970s, when Egypt made peace with Israel, the Palestinian Arabs knew that they would have to fight their own battle.

Divisions on Both Sides

Even among the Palestinians, however, people had different ideas about the goal of this continued struggle. Some people still wanted Israel's destruction, but an increasing number

Palestinian adults and children throw stones at Israeli police during demonstrations in Gaza in 1988.

realized that this was impractical.
These Palestinians felt that the best
they could hope for was a country of
their own in the West Bank and Gaza
Strip—the territories occupied by
Israel in 1967. Beyond this, Palestinians
held different opinions about how they
should conduct their struggle. Some
favored guerrilla warfare, some
terrorism. Others believed that only diplomacy would work.

Similarly, Israelis disagreed about how they should treat the
Palestinians and the disputed land. Some Israelis had very rigid
ideas about their goals. These "hard-liners"—like Menachem
Begin who became prime minister in 1977—wanted to keep all
of the original Palestine, and even add parts of Jordan,
Lebanon, and Syria. This, they claimed, was the original Land of
Israel. Seizing all of this territory was politically impossible, but
building more Jewish **settlements** in the occupied territories
was a way of preserving them for Israel's future. Other
Israelis—particularly those associated with the large Peace
Now movement—rejected this policy. It would be better, these
Israelis argued, to give up the occupied territories in exchange
for a lasting peace. Most Israelis fell between these two
extremes. They wanted peace, but they were not convinced that
the Palestinians were ready or willing to be peaceful neighbors.

Toward the Intifada

In 1974, the Palestine Liberation Organization (PLO) leader
Yasser Arafat made a historic speech. Speaking in New York,
he offered the Israelis a choice between "the olive branch and
the gun"—in other words, between peace and war. But Arafat
still refused to recognize the right of the state of Israel to exist,
and, because of this, the Israelis did not trust him. Once
Egypt and Israel made peace in 1979, the military threat
to Israel almost disappeared. As far as most Israelis were
concerned, there seemed no pressing need to negotiate with
the Palestinians. On the contrary, Israel continued building
settlements in the occupied territories and, in 1982, forced
the PLO out of Lebanon.

Illegal Settlements

"The occupying power shall
not deport or transfer parts
of its own civilian population
into the territory it occupies."

*Article 49 of the Geneva
Convention relative to the
Protection of Civilian Persons
in Times of War, which came
into force in October 1950.*

The Israelis hoped that the PLO and Arafat would become irrelevant and that more moderate leaders would emerge in the occupied territories. Unfortunately, Israel's policy in the territories—the confiscation of land for settlements, the seizure of scarce water resources, the heavy policing—increased Palestinian feelings of resentment and humiliation. On December 9, 1987, after four Palestinians had been knocked down and killed by an Israeli truck, a series of riots broke out. Soon, protests, riots, and violent events were occurring all over the occupied territories. The first Palestinian **intifada,** or uprising, had begun. For the next six years, it was featured frequently on TV news shows around the world, offering visual evidence of the often brutal clash.

Hopes of Peace

The intifada, and the Western pressure it produced, forced Israel to reconsider its policies. In 1993–1994 secret talks between Israeli officials and the PLO in Norway ended in agreement over the way forward. The two sides then openly recognized each other, and Israel agreed to let the Palestinians set up the Palestinian National Authority to run some of their own affairs.

Unfortunately, the Israeli prime minister most responsible for this breakthrough, Yitzhak Rabin, was murdered in 1995. When the next election was won by a hard-liner, Benjamin Netanyahu, the peace process was brought to a halt. His successor in 1998, Ehud Barak, tried again. Overall agreement was reached on the future of the West Bank—95 percent would belong to a new Palestinian country and the Palestinians would receive land elsewhere in Israel in exchange for the 5 percent that Israel kept. But the two sides failed to reach agreement on Jerusalem or on the rights of Palestinian refugees, and any hope of future progress was lost when Yasser Arafat walked out of the peace talks. Barak lost the Israeli election of February 2001 to Likud Party leader Ariel Sharon.

Just over four months earlier, on September 28, 2000, Sharon had visited the Temple Mount in Jerusalem, a site holy to both Jews and Muslims, accompanied by about 1,000 armed policemen. The visit was considered provocative by many

U.S. President Bill Clinton stands between Yasser Arafat (right) and Israeli Prime Minister Yitzhak Rabin as they shake hands in 1993. Rabin and Arafat had signed a historic agreement on Palestinian autonomy in the occupied territories. Rabin was assassinated two years later.

Palestinians. Violent clashes took place, and gradually spread through the occupied territories. These clashes marked the start of a second intifada, one which would feature frequent suicide bombings by Palestinian groups and frequent military responses by Israel's Air Force, both of which caused widespread civilian casualties.

As prime minister, Sharon abandoned dialogue with the Palestinians in favor of unilateral actions. In 2002, Israel began to construct a barrier between Israelis and those areas controlled by the Palestinian National Authority. Israel argued that the barrier was intended to provide security from terrorist attack. The Palestinians argued that the barrier represented a permanent border within Palestinian territory. In August 2005, Sharon ordered the removal of all 8,500 Jewish settlers from the Gaza Strip. About 400,000 remained in the West Bank.

Yasser Arafat had died the previous year and in 2005, Mahmoud Abbas was elected president of the Palestinian National Authority. Democratic elections held in the Palestinian National Authority in January 2006 resulted in a surprise victory for the radical group Hamas, a terrorist organization dedicated to the destruction of Israel. The Israeli government refused to deal with Hamas, as did many Western governments.

CHAPTER 7

The War on Terror

The so-called **War on Terror** is not confined to the Middle East. Its roots, however, lie in the long and frequently troubled relationship between the region's Muslims and the Western powers. A Middle Eastern conflict in its own right, it has also deeply affected already existing conflicts like those involving Iraq and Israel.

A Declaration of War

On September 11, 2001 a group of nineteen Islamic fundamentalists—fifteen of them from Saudi Arabia—hijacked four civilian airplanes in the United States. Two of the planes were flown into the twin towers of the World Trade Center in New York City; one was crashed into the Pentagon, headquarters of the U.S. Department of Defense. The fourth plane crashed in the Pennsylvania countryside after passengers overtook the hijackers. On the following day U.S. president George W. Bush announced a "War on Terror."

This war had in fact been underway for several years. It was not a war in the usual

Clouds of smoke rise from the site of the destruction of the World Trade Center Twin Towers. The Pentagon was also damaged that day.

sense, but it was certainly a conflict involving extreme violence. On one side were the world's governments, intelligence services, police forces, and armed services—or at least the vast majority of them. On the other side was a wide range of terrorist groups. Many groups on the terrorist side were Islamic fundamentalist groups. Many had some connection to the Islamic fundamentalist **umbrella group** known as al-Qaeda. It was al-Qaeda operatives who planned and executed the attacks on 9/11.

A New Enemy

"The American people need to know we are facing a different enemy than we have ever faced. This enemy hides in the shadows and has no regard for human life. This is an enemy who preys on innocent and unsuspecting people, then runs for cover. But it won't be able to run for cover forever ..."

President George W. Bush, speaking to the American people on September 12, 2001, the day after the al-Qaeda attacks on New York City and Washington, D.C.

The Rise of al-Qaeda

Osama bin Laden, a Saudi Arabian, founded al-Qaeda. His original intention was to form an international Islamic fighting force, made up of veterans of the Afghan war against the Soviets. These fighters would go wherever they were needed to defend and promote Islam. An original partner in this scheme was Abdullah Azzam, but Azzam was opposed to the use of terrorism. Azzam was killed in 1989, most probably by allies of bin Laden.

When Saddam invaded Kuwait and threatened Saudi Arabia in 1990, bin Laden offered twelve thousand of his fighters to the Saudi government. The government rejected the offer. It asked instead for help from the United States. This use of non-Muslims to defend Saudi Arabia and its holy places enraged bin Laden. He began to speak out against the Saudi government, leading to his expulsion from the country. The Saudi government and its Western allies became the main targets of the terrorist campaign that al-Qaeda began in the early 1990s. The organization also sent fighters to support the Muslim rebellions in the Russian republic of Chechnya and Kashmir, a territory disputed by India and Pakistan.

Bin Laden's Demands

"These events have divided the world into two camps, the camp of the faithful and the camp of the **infidels** [non-believers in Islam]. . . As to America, I say to it and its people a few words: I swear to Allah that those living in America will not live in security and safety until we live in peace and security in our lands and in Palestine, and the army of the infidels has departed from the land of Muhammad [Arabia], peace be upon him."

Osama bin Laden, al-Qaeda leader, speaking on a video issued by al-Jazeera TV a station based in Qatar on October 7, 2001.

A Hero to Some

What motivated bin Laden and his terrorist allies? No doubt personal ambition played a part, as did belief in fundamentalist Islamic ideology. Some people would say that al-Qaeda's leaders were driven by the evil in their hearts. This may have been partly true, but it was far from the whole truth. Like the Arab nationalists before them, the Islamic fundamentalists of al-Qaeda see themselves as responding to centuries of Western interference in their countries and their culture. And their assault on the West won them many Middle Eastern sympathizers. Many Middle Easterners were even prepared to look past the terrorist methods that bin Laden used. What was the difference, they asked, between killing American civilians with planes in New York and killing Iraqi civilians with bombings during and after the invasion of Iraq? It was a hard truth for most Westerners to swallow, but Osama bin Laden was a hero to many in the Middle East.

Unintended Consequences

After 9/11, the al-Qaeda leadership was forced to flee from its base in Afghanistan. Since then, the organization and its terrorist allies have launched murderous attacks in Bali, Madrid, London, and Amman. The attacks have killed many innocent people, but they have had little or no effect on Western policy. Al-Qaeda in Iraq's campaign of violence in post-Saddam Iraq, however, has made life very difficult for the occupation authorities and for Iraqi civilians working to rebuild their country.

After the war in Afghanistan, most experts believed that the next stage of the War on Terror would involve the hunting down of al-Qaeda. The Bush administration disagreed. Despite the lack of any evidence connecting al-Qaeda and Saddam Hussein, the Bush administration decided that removing Saddam would further the War on Terror. Many commentators suggested at the time that it seemed more likely to have the opposite effect. In fact, some Iraqi opponents of the post-Saddam occupation did welcome support from both homegrown and foreign al-Qaeda sympathizers. Ill-treatment of detainees has provided opponents of the occupation with propaganda victories. The continuing conflict in Iraq between the occupation forces and their opponents has become a battle for the hearts and minds of the whole Middle East.

U.S. marines conduct a street patrol to search for insurgents on November 10, 2004 in Fallujah, Iraq. The civilian deaths during the Fallujah campaign are still the object of intense criticism and debate.

CHAPTER 8

Future Conflicts

The sources of conflict in the Middle East have hardly changed in sixty years. Political differences, ethnic and religious differences, competition for natural resources, and foreign interference continue to play their part. The Arab world and Iran are still torn between Western-style modernization and a more Islamic version of political and economic development.

Towards a Pax Americana?

"The mission begins in Baghdad, but it does not end there. Were the United States to retreat after victory into complacency and self-absorption, as it did the last time it went to war in Iraq, new dangers would soon arise. Preventing this outcome will be a burden, of which the war in Iraq represents but the first installment. But America cannot escape its responsibility for maintaining a decent world order. The answer to this challenge is the American idea itself (of individual rights and freedoms), and behind it the unparalleled military and economic strength of the country. Duly armed, the United States can act to secure its safety and to advance the cause of liberty—in Baghdad and beyond."

Lawrence Kaplan and William Cristol, The War Over Iraq. *These two influential American journalists were among those who signed the famous letter sent to President Clinton in 1998.*

Ideology and Religion

Discontent is widespread in the oil-poor countries of the Middle East. The old Arab nationalist governments have failed to deliver economic development or real **democracy**. Millions of people are poor and unemployed. Not surprisingly, many of these people have turned to the Islamic parties and groups, in the hope that their recipes for economic and political progress prove more successful.

Discontent is also at a high level in Saudi Arabia, where the 22,000-strong

Iranian women walk on a
U.S. flag painted on a street
as they leave a polling
station in southern Tehran
in June 2005. The result
was a victory for hardliner
Mahmoud Ahmadinejad.

royal family
continues to enjoy
all of the political
power and much
of the country's oil-
generated wealth.
Since Saudi Arabia
is already an Islamic
fundamentalist
country in most
respects, opposition
to the government
may come from even
more extreme groups.

Iraq's Sunnis and Shi'as

Now that the civil war
in Lebanon is over, Iraq has become the only state that is
seriously divided by ethnic and religious differences. When
Saddam was overthrown, seventy years of rule by the country's
Sunni Muslim minority came to an end. The Shi'a majority
now makes up the largest group in the central government,
and the Kurdish minority enjoy a semi-independent status
in their own areas. The Sunnis are now resisting both foreign
occupation and Shi'a rule. The situation could be resolved by
the creation of a working federal democracy, and the high turn-
out in recent elections has offered hope that this may come to
pass. However, civil war remains a real possibility.

The American Build-Up

Saddam's removal from power was a warning to other ambitious, anti-American dictators. Libya's President Gaddafi got the message. He stopped his support for terrorism and promised not to develop weapons of mass destruction.

Access to secure sources of oil has grown more important in recent years, as prices rise and oil reserves shrink. Many analysts see this as the main reason for the steady build-up of American forces in the Middle East after the first Gulf War. There are now U.S. bases in Saudi Arabia, Oman, the United Arab Emirates (UAE), Qatar, Kuwait, and, of course, Iraq. Other U.S. bases are scattered around the fringes of the Middle Eastern region, in Turkey, Djibouti, Kyrgyzstan, Tajikistan, Afghanistan, and Pakistan. Some commentators say this large and growing foreign military presence has reminded Middle Easterners of their own lowly status in the world, encouraged the growth of anti-Western feelings, and become a source of conflict in its own right.

A left-wing Israeli activist from Peace Now shouts during a protest in Halhul, near the West Bank town of Hebron, in October 2005. The group was protesting Jewish settlements in the divided West Bank town of Hebron.

The U.S. build-up has particularly alarmed the Islamic Republic of Iran. Already condemned by President George W. Bush in 2002 as part of an "Axis of Evil" for its alleged support for terrorist organizations, the country now finds itself surrounded by U.S. military bases. Accusations that Iran is secretly building nuclear weapons—and Israeli threats of military action if they are—have added to the tension. The recent election of Islamic hardliner Mahmoud Ahmadinejad to the Iranian presidency, and his speech in October 2005 calling for the destruction of Israel, have caused great concern in the international community. There have been calls for economic sanctions against Iran, and military action against Iran by either the United States or Israel remains a possibility.

No Solution

"Israel is becoming a graveyard of children. The Holy Land is being turned into a wasteland. If an Israeli child is killed, and the next day a Palestinian child is killed, it's no solution."

Nurit and Rami Elhanan, Israeli parents who lost their 14-year-old daughter in a Palestinian suicide bombing. From John King's Israel and Palestine *[Oxford: Heinemann Library, 2005].*

A Stubborn Problem

It is now sixty years since Britain handed the problem of Palestine over to the United Nations, and still no solution is in sight. The conflict contains all the typical Middle Eastern elements. It was set in motion by foreign meddling. It features two communities separated by religion and culture—one rich by Middle Eastern standards, one dreadfully poor. It involves competition for natural resources—in this case, land and water. Rather less typically, it seems clear that this problem can only be solved by more pressure from Western governments and the governments of other nations in the region on the chief protagonists—Israel and the Palestinian National Authority. The March 2006 election in Israel saw the new Kadima party of the ailing Ariel Sharon emerge as the strongest force in Israeli politics. Dedicated to granting land concessions to the Palestinians, Kadima now has to contend with a Palestinian National Authority dominated by Hamas, under Prime Minister Ismail Haniya. It remains to be seen whether the present impasse can ever be breached.

1914–1918 World War I.

1917   Balfour Declaration.

1920   Britain given mandates to rule Palestine, Transjordan, and Iraq; France given mandate to rule Syria (including future Lebanon). Nationalist uprising against British rule erupts in Iraq.

1922   Egypt is given formal independence.

1932   Iraq is given formal independence.

1939–1945 World War II.

1945–1947 Violence escalates in Palestine.

1947   United Nations (UN) partitions Palestine.

1947–1948 Fighting in Palestine.

1948   State of Israel is founded.

1948–1949 First Arab-Israeli War.

1950s   Arab guerrillas mount raids into Israel from Egypt.

1951–1953 Conflict between Iranian Prime Minister Mossadegh and the Western powers ends with Mossadegh's overthrow.

1952   Free Officer revolution in Egypt.

1956   Nasser's nationalization of the Suez Canal sparks the Suez Crisis.

1958   Iraqi officers overthrow pro-British regime in Baghdad.

1960   Organization of Petroleum Exporting Countries (OPEC) is founded.

1962–1967 War of independence in Aden Protectorate (South Yemen).

1962–1970 Civil war in North Yemen.

1963–1975 Civil war in Oman.

1967   (June) Second Arab-Israeli War.

1970   Black September in Jordan.

1973   (October) Third Arab-Israeli War.

1974   Yasser Arafat makes "Gun and Olive Branch" speech in New York.

1975–1991 Lebanese Civil War.

1977   Menachem Begin becomes prime minister of Israel.

1978–1996 Afghan civil wars.

1979   (January) Iranian revolution. (March) Peace treaty between Egypt and Israel. (June) Saddam Hussein becomes president of Iraq. (December) Soviets intervene in Afghanistan.

1979–1980 Libyan forces mount military interventions in Chad and Tunisia.

1980–1982 Virtual civil war in Iran.

1980–1988 Iran-Iraq War.

1982   Israel invades Lebanon.

1987–1988 Osama bin Laden founds al-Qaeda.

1987–1993 First intifada.

1990   Iraq invades Kuwait; Osama bin Laden's offer of military assistance is rejected by the Saudi Arabian government.

1991   UN coalition forces Iraq out of Kuwait.

1993–1994 Secret talks between Israel and the PLO take place in Oslo, Norway.

1994   Establishment of Palestinian National Authority.

1996   Taliban takes Afghan capital Kabul.

2001   (February) Ariel Sharon becomes prime minister of Israel. (September) 9/11 attacks on the United States; the War on Terror is declared.

2002   President George W. Bush claims there is an "Axis of Evil" that includes Iraq, Iran, and North Korea.

2003   Saddam Hussein is overthrown by United States-led invasion; violent resistance to occupation of Iraq begins.

2005   Israel withdraws settlements from Gaza Strip.

GLOSSARY

Arab nationalist: a person who believes in the development of an increasingly united Arab world

Ba'athist: an Arab nationalist who advocates pan-Arab socialism; the Ba'ath party rules Syria and used to rule Iraq until the fall of Saddam Hussein

Balfour Declaration: the letter written by British Foreign Minister Arthur Balfour in 1917 that promised British help in creating a Jewish national home in Palestine

Christianity: one of the world's three major monotheistic (one-God) religions.

civil war: war between different groups in the same country

colonial: concerning the rule of economically underdeveloped countries by economically advanced countries

conservatives: (in the Middle East) people who believe that Westernization and modernization threaten traditional Islamic values; conservatives in the Middle East are suspicious of democratic systems of government.

democracy: the political system in which governments are freely elected by the people, or a country in which this system exists

dictator: an individual who rules on his or her own, unrestricted by others

diplomacy: management of relations between countries by peaceful means

economic sanctions: policies of refusing to trade with a particular country, either in one particular product or in all products, as a way of forcing that country into compliance

ethnic: relating to different tribal, racial, cultural, or linguistic groups

guerrilla: an unofficial or irregular soldier

hijack: to forcefully take over a vehicle

Holocaust: the mass murder of European Jews by the German Nazis during World War II; it is estimated that about six million Jews died during the Holocaust.

illiteracy: inability to read or write

infidels: people who don't believe in God; name that some Muslims give to those who do not believe in their Islamic God

intelligence services: government agencies that gather secret information about other countries

intifada: Arabic word meaning "uprising"

Islam: one of the world's three major monotheistic (one God) religions, founded by the Prophet Muhammad in the seventh century

Islamic fundamentalist: a person who believes in following a very strict interpretation of Islam

Judaism: one of the world's three major monotheistic (one-God) religions

mandate rule: rule that has been authorized by international agreement

Mesopotamian provinces: the land between the Tigris and Euphrates rivers, now known as Iraq

militia: a non-professional unit of fighters

GLOSSARY

modernization: the updating of a country's economy, using the latest ideas and technology

nationalists: people who put their own nation above all others

neoconservatives: (in the United States) politicians who believe that the United States should actively promote its interests in foreign countries

oppression: keeping down

Ottoman Empire: the empire of the Ottoman Turks, which lasted over 600 years (1299-1922), and which included all of the Middle East except Iran and the desert interior of the Arabian Peninsula

Palestinian National Authority: the government of those areas of the occupied territories given limited self-rule in 1994

partition: divide up

persecution: being picked out for cruel treatment

personality cult: a view of a government leader as an ideal person and as a perfect leader

refugee: a person who, for various reasons, has been forced to leave his or her own country

separatist: devoted to having a separate country in what is currently part of an established country

settlements: newly established communities; in the occupied territories, Israeli communities established since 1967

shah: Iranian word for "emperor"

Shi'a: Muslims who believe the rightful leaders of Islam are the descendants of Muhammad's son-in-law Ali.

slavery: ownership of other human beings

Suez Canal Zone: the strip of territory on either side of the Suez Canal. The canal, which lies wholly within Egyptian territory, enormously shortens the sea route from the Persian Gulf to Europe and North America.

Sunnis: Muslims who accept the first four caliphs as rightful leaders of Islam

terrorism: violence used to intimidate people for political reasons

umbrella group: a group that coordinates the actions of many other groups

United Nations (UN): the international body set up in 1945 to promote peace and cooperation between countries

UN weapons inspectors: inspectors sent by the UN to make sure that a country has destroyed its prohibited weapons

War on Terror: the worldwide campaign to eliminate terrorism that began in September 2001, after the September 11 terrorist attacks on the United States

weapons of mass destruction: nuclear, chemical, and biological weapons

Westernization: the adoption of Western ideas, technologies, and cultural values

Yom Kippur: the most solemn holy day of the year for Jews, known as the Day of Atonement, and spent in fasting and prayer

Zionist: a person who advocates the creation of a Jewish country in Palestine

Web Sites

BBC News: Middle East
    http://news.bbc.co.uk/1/hi/world/middle_east/
CNN International: World/Middle East
    http://edition.cnn.com/WORLD/meast/archive
History in the News: Middle East
    http://www.albany.edu/history/middle-east/
Politics: From Royalty to Democracy
    http://www.pbs.org/wgbh/globalconnections/mideast/themes/
    politics/

Note to educators and parents: The publisher has carefully reviewed these Web sites to ensure that they are suitable for children. Many Web sites change frequently, however, and Gareth Stevens, Inc., cannot guarantee that a site's future contents will continue to meet our high standards of quality and educational value. Be advised that children should be closely supervised whenever they access the Internet.

Books

Gaag, Nikki, von der and Felicity Arbuthnot. *Baghdad* (Great Cities of the World). World Almanac Library, 2006.

King, John. *Iran and the Islamic Revolution* (The Middle East). Raintree, 2005.

Uschan, Michael. *Suicide Bombings in Israel and Palestinian Terrorism* (Terrorism in Today's World). World Almanac Library, 2006.

Woolf, Alex. *The Arab-Israeli Conflict* (Atlas of Conflicts). World Almanac Library, 2005.

ABOUT THE AUTHOR

David Downing has been writing books for adults and children about political, military, and cultural history for thirty years. He has written several books on the modern Middle East. He has lived in the United States and traveled extensively in Asia, Africa, and Latin America. He now resides in Britain.

ABOUT THE CONSULTANT

William Ochsenwald is Professor of History at Virginia Polytechnic Institute and State University. He is author of *The Middle East: A History*, a textbook now in its sixth edition. Professor Ochsenwald has also written many other books and articles dealing with the history of the Middle East.

INDEX

APR 15 2009

31⁰⁰